BREAKING THE spirit of Solomon (the apostate)

by
evangelist Oleg MB

Understanding down fall
of Most powerful Monarch
is the key for the keepers
of the Name!!!!

failure has pattern
do you know it?

Contents

Introduction

Who was Solomon?

King Solomon was the wisest king: wealth, temple, books, force and women.,.., these well summarizes his life in a nutshell.

This is my approach is not that of teacher but of scribe that is meticulous, scrupulous and splitting hair person just as Jesus said: “not even one iota.....”

Chapter I
Misappropriation of wealth

Israel was supposed to be the light and bring knowledge of God to all nations. All nations was supposed to look at Israel and come to the knowledge of True and living God. That is why God spoke in **Deuteronomy 8:18:**

Remember the Lord your God, for that is he who gives you power to get wealth.

AWESOME!!!!!!!!

For what reason?

So he can establish his covenant w you- i.e. purpose of wealth. Purpose of wealth was so that covenant be established.

So when Solomon came to full power and got wealth. What happened? He lost purpose for the wealth that he got. "not the half has been told...." -

1Kings 10: 1And when the queen of Sheba heard of the fame of Solomon concerning the name of the LORD, she came to prove him with hard questions.(she came concerning the name of the Lord.. please notice

that) 2And she came to Jerusalem with a very great
train, with camels that bare spices, and very much gold,
and precious stones: and when she was come to Solomon,
she communed with him of all that was in her heart.3And
Solomon told her all her questions: there was not *any* thing
hid from the king, which he told her not.(did he tell
her about holiness, Yeshua, purpose of
wealth, father of faith Abraham, the joy
of salvation, restoration of right spirit;
folks we are not talking about dummy
here, but the wisest king, yes really,
really you Solomon told her everything
but what you should have told her) 4And
when the queen of Sheba had seen all Solomon's wisdom,
and the house that he had built, 5And the meat of his table,
and the sitting of his servants, and the attendance of his
ministers, and their apparel, and his cupbearers, and his
ascent by which he went up unto the house of the LORD;
there was no more spirit in her(watch this, what
about to restore the right spirit within
me or her in that case : this was perfect
occasion for exchange of her gods for
one true God. 6And she said to the king, It was a true
report that I heard in mine own land of thy acts and of thy
wisdom. 7Howbeit I believed not the words, until I came,(

the woman was ready to get saved, get converted, to give whatever she needed to give up to gain what Solomons God had to offer and that son of the David failed royalty!!!- he Solomon himself wrote he who wins souls is wise …. Did you win the soul Solomon or you let that fish slip... my my and mine eyes had seen *it*: and, behold, the half was not told me: thy wisdom and prosperity exceedeth the fame which I heard.

There are many other scriptures that I can pull up. But why waste ink. Do your own research my dear reader So as you my dear reader can see that obviously that Solomon didn't appropriate his wealth to establish the covenant.,,

II
Presence of God

My people perish for the lack of knowledge ….. where there is no vision..or prophetic involvement.people perish.

Solomon was the wisest king on the earth. Had access to Jewish history, books fathers library and many other classified information that the king of his caliber would have.

Yet, no presence of God in the form of seers, prophets, dream interpreters was desired, pursued or wisely sought after. The general presence of God was not a big concern of his.

The words of his own father : _"cast me not from thy presence all Lord!!!!!.......... restore the right spirit within me............ renew the joy of my salvation......."_ mind you those are the words of his father David.

Presence of God through tumim and Urim. Yes he built temple and yes I am not talking about Solomon in his very beginnings though even his beginnings were not to hot either.

Instead of pursuing God he had other agendas, look at these scriptures"

no amassing of horses, no multiplying of wives, and no accumulating of silver and gold (Deuteronomy 17:14-20). Instead of pursuing God and seeking his face through fasting, prayer, prophetic, umim and turim, visions, and dreams, interpreters of dreams.

Mind you he started in the presence of God and sought God the most High and was found by him: God answered him in and by the dream.

But unfortunately it was just a spark that never started any fire... he was floating on his God given wisdom and spoiled it anyway as further we will see in this booklet . As life went on and his fame and kingdom grew look what happened:

"As Solomon grew old, his wives turned his heart after other gods, and his heart was not fully devoted to the LORD his God" (1 Kings 11:4).

But if that was not enough and was not bad enough look what he does next. Wow what a terrible statement:

To please his wives, Solomon even got involved in sacrificing to Milcom (or Molech), a god that required "detestable" acts to be performed (1 Kings 11:7-8).

if one does not seek God he by default will do his thing. This was not a little sin, **this was total apostasy**

to sacrifice to other gods. The important note is that priest were there and temple was there. Worship of God was there, but so what? So were other gods present at the the same time. To the degree that there was one temple to God almighty and hundred to the so called gods.

There was no prophet to rebuke, there was no vision, dreams, or any other signs and wonders to miracles to stop Solomons foolishness.

That is tragedy. **<u>Solomon your own father said:</u>** "your visitation ohh Lord has preserved my spirit" . God presence makes all the difference.

No presence of God – no God.

The Temple of the Lord , the Temple of the Lord …… thats what people kept saying.

Chapter III

Diminished passover!!!!!!

what about passover? Passover in OT was the festival and feast to keep and yet what do we see w Solomon.

Passover was the key element in redemptive act that God has performed while delivering Israel from out of Egypt. Passover was about the Lamb, no Lamb no Passover. Now, we know that the Lamb is Jesus.
No passover no Jesus, no Jesus no redemption. So to

me Passover is associated w redemption and Messiah.

OK, OK you might say what does this have to do with Solomon?
2Kings 23:22 and
2Chronicles 35:18;
wow!!!!!!

Now we know big shot Solomon – but who is this no name Josiah?????

2 Chronicles 35 (KJV)

35 Moreov**er Josiah kept a passover** (who was this king Josiah?????) unto the Lord in Jerusalem: **2** And he set the priests in their charges, and encouraged them to the service of the house of the Lord,**3** And said unto the Levites that taught all Israel, which were holy unto the Lord, Put the holy

ark in the h**ouse which Solomon the son of David
king of Israel did build;** (What?? there it
is Solomon mentioned!!!! but why
did not Solomon celebrated
Passover, why???) 4 And prepare yourselves
by the houses of your fathers, after your courses,
according to the writing of David king of Israel, and
according to the writing of Solomon his son.
(what? What? Ohh Solomon
mentioned again, but in all his glory
Solomon never dared to celebrate
the Passover or Jesus to the degree
that Josiah did? Why???) 6 So kill the
passover, and sanctify yourselves, and prepare your
brethren, that they may do according to the word of
the Lord by the hand of Moses.

7 And **Josiah gave to the people,** of the flock, lambs
and kids, all for the passover offerings, for all that
were present, to the number of thirty thousand, and
three thousand bullocks: these were of the king's
substance. 8 And **his princes gave willingl**y unto the
people, to the priests, rulers of the house of God, gave
unto the priests for the passover offerings two

thousand and six hundred small cattle and three
hundred oxen. 9 gave unto the Levites for passover
offerings five thousand small cattle, and five hundred
oxen. 11 And they **killed the passover, and the
priests sprinkled the blood from their hands, and
the Levites flayed them.** 12 , as it is written in the
book of Moses. (SO Solomon didn't do
what is written in the book of
Moses???? obviously not)13 And they
**roasted the passover with fire according to the
ordinance:** but the other holy offerings. 15 **And the
singers the sons of Asaph were in their place,
according to the commandment of David, and
Asaph, and Heman, and Jeduthun the king's seer;
and the porters waited at every gate; they might
not depart from their service;** for their brethren the
Levites prepared for them. **16 So all the service of
the Lord was prepared the same day, to keep the
passove**r, according to the commandment of king
Josiah.17 **And the children of Israel that were
present kept the passover at that time, and the
feast of unleavened bread seven days**.

With less money Josiah did more than Solomon

With less glory Josiah did more than Solomon

With less power Josiah did more than Solomon

God will choose foolish things of the world to confine the wise ....

Josiah confound Solomon – big time!!!!!!!!!!!

And here is the key, or corner stone of proof that Solomon has failed in celebrating the passover or the blood of Jesus.

Read next verse... and keep in mind the mangnitude of Solomon and mini kingdom of Josiah, and preacher you mean to tell me that Josiah overshadowed Solomon, yes !!!!!!! read this verse :

18 And there was no passover like to that kept in Israel from the days of Samuel the prophet; neither did all the kings of Israel keep such a passover as Josiah kept, and the priests, and the Levites, and all Judah and Israel that were present, and the inhabitants of Jerusalem.

Solomon:
Wise but not self aware.
Scriptures:
"the spirit of the man is the candle of the Lord..."
and
"if the light that is in you is darkness- how big is that darkness???"

In my humble experience of as of 2015 will be quarter of the century in church ministry. (Solomon was magnetized by the women that worshiped demons. He awareness was occupied w the bodies of women of all kinds.)

I have noticed one perplexing truth. One can know God but have no clue about who he is or she is. One can know about Jesus and what he has done for you: but would have no clue who they are, what they are supposed to do and what life is all about. One person can be so into God that has forgotten the location of God that she or he is so into.

One person can know all truth about God but if he does not know himself – that knowledge of God would not do him any good. It is like having a computer but don't know how to turn it on, use it, and make it productive machinery for its designed purpose. (see my other booklets for that)

So it was w Solomon; his person was extremely wise he was so into God of wisdom and wisdom that he forgot about himself. How to care for his soul. I mean that his body houses God; His being houses the wisdom of God. But that does not mean that all wisdom that he houses: Solomon knows hot to use it, or apropriates all the wisdom he is got. This is the Key.

Solomon was not aware of who he is or how to do things in accordance to the gift of wisdom that he is gotten as a gift from God. I am not trying to harp on his imperfections OK,.,. I am just letting you know what thus sayeth the Lord,..,

Using Doctors diagnosis that Luke has made based on how Holy Ghost determined to say through him. Lets consider this verse. And you tell me all you know so far about Solomon; what does that should mean or tell me about Solomon and Sheba.

Luke 12:27

Consider the lilies how they grow: they toil not, they spin not; and yet I say unto you, that

Solomon in all his glory was not arrayed like one of these.

God chose to put that verse here. It seems like It is nitty gritty matter. Well when you go to your doctor (let him use wrong knife to cut you open or give you wrong prescription- cause he does not want to be nitty gritty)

So Sheba was so impressed with apparel of Solomon- realy, you mean to tell me she was impressed out her mind. That she didn't realize that lily was dressed higher than Solomon.

Luke states that lily was dressing better than Solomon , yes I looked at all theologians.(not that I need their approval- but it was for the sake of you- my reader who god is your reason- repent,but anyway: guess what they give their theories along these lines.

"Solomon in all of his glory was not dressed like those lilies....." - all of his glory, all – all of his glory and yet lower than lily.

Many mistake wisdom for selfawarness. **Solomon was wise but not self aware.** Person can function at its best as the king but not be self aware. **He knew wisdom but he did not know himself.** He was a Chanel through whom Gods wisdom flow out of. But that was is. Nothing remained in him to make him self aware. Wisdom is not the same as self awareness. So it was w Solomon. He was so wise but not selfaware that he dressed below the standard of the lily. Lily was true to its nature more than Solomon was to his nature, why because he was not self aware of his own true self

He was not self aware of who he realy was. He was not conscious of his true nature. He had knowledge of wisdom but not self knowledge. Person can act and behave like they are on cruise control. Our without putting their mind to it. It is like second nature to them.

So it was w Solomon .

Not to recognize that you are dressing yourself below the lily. **<u>Knowing how to dress above the level of lily is self knowledge.</u>**

Self awareness of how to dress , dressing yourself is very basic principle of life, and Solomon dressed below the lily. Not even on the level of the flower. Being self aware is using that candle of the Lord.

Solomon was magnetized by the women that worshiped demons. He awareness was occupied w the bodies of women of all kinds.

How can you know wisdom if you don't know yourself? You can , ones imperfections can not and will not distort ultimate truth. Wisdom does not equal self awareness, just like any other craft. Too many scriptures but look at book of Ecclesiastes, this book will tell you about how conscious Solomon was about himself. And how much selfawarness he had about himself.

Lily was more self aware and self conscious than Solomon.

V
What wisdom?

I would like to make sure you understand – I do believe that in the beginnings Solomon as I called him the Alpha Solomon was good and God truly gave him wisdom. But as the life went on and Solomon became more corrupt and so became the way in which he treated

the most precious wisdom. Gift of wisdom from God was awesome and pure but the way that Solomon treated it has many implication, hence the title to this concluding chapter : What wisdom ?
In epistle of James chapter 3 it states :

3:15-18

15 [1]This wisdom is not that which descends from [a]above, but is [2]earthly, [b]soulish, [c]demonic.

16 For where jealousy and selfish ambition are, there [a]disorder and every worthless practice are.

17 But the [1a]wisdom from above is first [b]pure, then [c]peaceable, [2]forbearing, [3]compliant, full of [d]mercy and good [e]fruit, [f]impartial, [g]without hypocrisy.

So what wisdom? Do you have when you have 1000 sexual encounters w women, so what wisdom do you have what wisdom do you have: when you allow your so called women to worship demons in Jerusalem the city of God?

So what wisdom do you have when you construction projects for idolatrous temples. So these women can sacrifice and burn incense to their gods=devils? What wisdom?? tell me shall I go on?

Numerous other hideous abominations were acted out and performed by backsliden, outmind, deceived, led astray, open minded Solomon. What wisdom? In the beginning it was God kind of Wisdom, that wisdom has made it to canon of the Bible.

Solomon instead talking about hidden wisdom 1Cor2:4 – instead of revealing Christ, God, mission, scientific discoveries. He ended up, talking about ants, pigs, wine, and other less important subject.

Solomon never explained the mystery of fall- but he could.

Solomon never explained the giants in Gen 6. but he could

Solomon never explained the tower of Babel but he could.

Solomon never explained how his dad David killed the Goliath – but he could

Solomon never explained the wisdom that was hidden from the foundation of the world but he could..

Solomon never explained how exactly Moses received the Law. But he could Solomon had most precious commodity at his disposal yet used it for lower purposes that for what it was originally intended.

Conclusion:

Obviously I barely scratched the surface- w intention that you my reader would do due diligence and further the study by prayer and fasting so you can install this mystery of how to break the spirit of Solomon in your area of influence.

Side note:
God showed mercy to Solomon for David's sake, but Solomon's kingdom was eventually divided. Another chastisement upon Solomon was war with theEdomitesand Aramians.

INVITATION:

Invitation:
"giving and receiving"
Cup of Cold water
to a prophet.
469 450 6743

evangelistoleg@
gmail.com
for more information

www.ingramcontent.com/pod-product-compliance
Ingram Content Group UK Ltd.
Pitfield, Milton Keynes, MK11 3LW, UK
UKHW041903190726
13854UKWH00003B/1065